T0359173

Rick Morton has bee
for over 14 years. His first book, *One Hundred Years of Dirt*, was shortlisted for the 2019 Victorian Premier's Literary Awards and the 2019 National Biography Award, longlisted for the 2018 Walkley Book of the Year, and longlisted for both Biography of the Year and the Matt Richell Award for New Writer of the Year at the 2019 ABIA Awards. Rick is the winner of the 2013 Kennedy Award for Young Journalist of the Year and the 2017 Kennedy Award for Outstanding Columnist. In 2019, Rick left *The Australian* where he worked as the social affairs writer with a particular focus on social policy and is now a Senior Reporter for *The Saturday Paper*.

Writers in the *On Series*

Rick Morton

On Money

hachette
AUSTRALIA

Published in Australia and New Zealand in 2020
by Hachette Australia
(an imprint of Hachette Australia Pty Limited)
Level 17, 207 Kent Street, Sydney NSW 2000
www.hachette.com.au

10 9 8 7 6 5 4 3 2 1

 A catalogue record for this
book is available from the
National Library of Australia

ISBN: 978 0 7336 4576 1 (paperback)

Cover design by Luke Causby, Blue Cork
Text design by Alice Graphics
Typeset by Kirby Jones
Printed and bound in Australia by McPherson's Printing Group

 The paper this book is printed on is
certified against the Forest Stewardship
Council® Standards. McPherson's Printing
Group holds FSC® chain of custody
certification SA-COC-005379. FSC® promotes environmentally
responsible, socially beneficial and economically viable
management of the world's forests.

To everyone who ever loaned me money, thank you:

Candice, Kylie, Bridie, Michael, Sammy C, Shannon, Anna, Alice, Fitz, Lana, SJ, Gini, Sanjan, Lauryn, Mum, Ash, Ben D, Meersy, Tony, Jo, Sabina and Monica.

The longest relationship I have ever had was with my debt collector, Lee, who got married and witnessed the birth of his first child during the years he was assigned to recover the money I owed on my credit card.

I owed Credit Corp money while I was still pretending to be straight and I continued to owe them money after coming out as gay. Lee was in friendly pursuit of me for longer than the term of any prime minister since John Howard.

And for what? $2500 granted to me by Westpac when I was eighteen years old and a first-year newspaper cadet, living on my own in a city for the first time in my life on $450 a week.

Because I had nothing to fall back on, not just no family money but a family with no money – and there is a difference – I would trot down to the ATM each week when my pay came in and withdraw every last dollar.

They couldn't take the money I needed to live off if I took it out of the bank first.

Oh, I knew the automatic payments would still come out and I would be penalised, but that was a problem for future Rick, a man who did not yet exist in the world of present-tense Rick and was therefore a perfect stranger.

This commitment to perfect present tense made for a perfectly tense present as each new day revealed the mistakes of the one before it.

But it was a way of surviving and it often gave me and Lee, who were building a strange kind of friendship, something to talk about when he would phone and ask why I had never made the repayments upon which we had just agreed.

On paper, I was broke, but in real life ... I was also broke.

This was nothing new, we had grown up that way, but for the first time in my life the stress was mine to carry on my own.

Most days, my bank balance was so deep into negative territory that zero felt like a victory. It is not fun to have nothing and it is more unnerving to know the precise volume of the nothing you have.

Bar my closest friend, everyone I knew in those years of scarcity had come from comfortable homes, if not obscene wealth, and they moved through the world as if held aloft on a cushion of air.

It's not that these people did not have problems, but their problems were different to mine. They were worried about people who wanted to eat the rich and I thought 'the rich' was a type of hors d'oeuvre. To the extent that they worried about money, it was on account of their investments in the stock market or potential insider trading charges. My concerns were more practical: Did I have enough money for the bus? Will I get kicked out of my house for not making rent? Do distant fathers just have poor spatial awareness?

And yet, as a destitute new adult, I was earning almost as much right then as my mum had earned for all her life while raising three children on her own. Her poverty was structural; mine, a combination of the system and the psychology it bred in me, the way a firestorm creates its own weather system.

I am still fighting the habits of a poor boy who grew into a middle-class man with no safety net. My friends look at me now with practised despair and say: 'Fuck, you are so terrible with money.'

And I still want to tell them: 'Yes, but I was worse without it.'

You know, they say money can't buy you happiness. Which is a lot like saying bipartisan action on climate change can't pay down the mortgage on our collective futures. Of course it can't, it doesn't exist. Money is a voluntary, mass illusion that we have created to make the ordinary transactions of living easier. In times only recently past, we used coins with actual value, or shells with cosmetic value, to buy the things we wanted. Nobody was out there telling West Africans using cowrie shells as currency that crustaceans couldn't buy them happiness. If somebody had, they would have asked for directions to the happiness store, as well they should.

Money is a means to an end.

And these transactions are themselves very real. A person with children to feed and no home may not be automatically happy when he is able to feed his children and rent a home, but the conditions for that happiness to exist are now much more ripe.

Researchers often cast their minds back to the evolution of first life on Earth. What were the necessary conditions? Carbon, oxygen in the atmosphere, water on the surface and high energy in the form of lightning in storms.

Now, remove any one or two of those and ask the question: was it happy? No. Because it never lived. First, we must live.

In human terms, shelter and nourishment are two of the key planks of a multi-plank strategy I like to call not being dead.

And here's the kicker: having a place to live and sustenance for the people you love will give you something that is even more precious. It will give you time.

This is an important realisation.

One of the key implications of Einstein's general theory of relativity is that time is not only real but also linked to space and is different for different people depending on the gravitational force they feel. The more gravity acts on a person, the less time they experience. To be clear, it isn't just the case that you perceive time to be slower. It *is* slower for you.

In this way, money is like gravity. It can slow time if you have enough of it. Money will give you every advantage, every accumulated possibility, and to have a critical mass of it is a manipulation of the clock.

Importantly, Einstein also showed that gravity isn't strictly a force created by large bodies like the planet Earth but is what happens when our natural state, which is to fall freely through space, is interrupted by the curvature of space-time created by any object. If you were stuck in an elevator that suddenly gave out, you will enter your natural state of freefall. In essence, this is the same as simply switching gravity off.

That's why acceleration is the same as gravity. As Einstein discovered, similarly with time, if you are accelerating – for example, in the elevator that is going up – you don't just feel heavier. You *are* heavier. In this sense, the

Earth is the elevator. It is getting in the way of us falling freely through space. But because space and time are the same, space is relative, too. It really, really is.

If you travelled to a star that is twenty-five light-years away from Earth at 99 per cent the speed of light, your friends back on Earth would watch you leave and slightly more than fifty years will have passed by the time you come back. But two things are materially different when you are on that spaceship. When you check the distance again while on the ship you'll find the star is only three-and-a-half light-years from Earth. So it's only going to take you seven years to complete the round trip. Really. You will need seven years' worth of water and food. You could watch seven years' worth of television. If you left at age twenty, you would be twenty-seven on your return. But your friends, who were the same age when you left, would be a little older than seventy.

As it happens, we are all travelling at the speed of light through space-time. When we are sitting down, we are not moving through space at all so all of that speed is transferred to our passage through time. But the faster we move through space, the more we take away from time. You can slow your passage through time by moving in space.

Like gravity, we must think of money as a force that acts on us. It can and does distort time and space. In the most crucial of ways, we can slow the passage of time with money.

We can allow ourselves to breathe. It is a lubricant, reducing the friction of existence.

My mum turned sixty last year but I know from my own observations that she is an old sixty. Genetics plays a part, certainly, but so does struggle. Her joints have seized from lifting and scraping and effort, effort, effort. Her mind wears the weariness of never quite knowing if things are going to turn out okay. If there will be money to pay the bills, the mental arithmetic involved in every hour of each day to figure out how. To have few financial resources is, at its most fundamental, to not always know how.

We are highly evolved apes. When we moved from the trees to the wide-open savannahs to become hunters we slowed down the maturation of our own young so that their brains could grow bigger for years after they were born. We couldn't fit the head of a twenty-five year old through the birth canal, and nor would, I'd suggest, either mum or newborn wish to experience it. So we took an extraordinary risk, to be defenceless for so many years but for the protection of our social group, in order to supercharge our own brains. Why did we do this?

To figure out how. How to hunt as a group; how to build tools that gave us an advantage over natural carnivore predators; and how to better survive the elements.

We need to know how. Do you have any idea what it means to the human brain to not be able to know this? To be constantly figuring? To put in the work and the cognitive horsepower and still be limited by, of all things, money, the very thing that didn't exist when we first unlocked the power of our own minds?

It is exhausting.

The human brain accounts for about 2–3 per cent of the body's total weight. But, on average, it consumes 25 per cent of the body's energy when it is at rest. So this is not merely a thought experiment. There is a very real cognitive tax levied on the impoverished brain.

So it is true, then, to say that money can't buy us happiness. But it can and does eliminate the stresses of our own existence. It is a force that acts on us. If you earn $500,000 a year and you are not happy, we can eliminate lack of resources as the animating force behind your condition. If you are destitute and unhappy, I will bet you London to a brick that, in almost every case, removing the stress of that penury will help. It won't make you happy but it will buy you the time and space to figure out what it is that makes you happy. Money is a force that gives us time and space, two relative substances just as they are under Einstein's theory.

I suspect there is diminishing value to the money a person earns or accrues once the basics are taken care of. In only the last year, for the first time in my adult life, I have been able to live without constantly checking my bank balance. After a dinner recently, my friend Tom texted to make sure I'd received his bank transfer for his share of the meal. I honestly didn't know because I hadn't looked in over a week.

That I could go an entire week without checking whether I had enough money to make purchases was revolutionary. A daily stress had gone. It was like discovering the nitrous oxide toggle on a street car in *Fast and the Furious*. I had more time, more energy, more power. Scarier still was how smoothly that transition had happened. There was no fanfare or celebration; my life shifted gears from somewhat comfortable to mostly comfortable. Intellectually, I had not even clocked the change that had happened until Tom texted me and I was forced to confront what had transformed around me.

How easy it is to forget what was so only a week before. Honestly, I felt younger.

Poverty, then, is not just a cognitive tax. It exacts a price on our bodies. I look at my mum, Deb, and see someone who has been robbed of time. On account of her low socio-economic status, she is also somebody who has been robbed more than once in actual home burglaries. That's not to say that poor people are more likely to be criminals, but that poor people are more likely to be victims of all kinds of violence, institutional or otherwise. And what crimes we do commit tend to be crimes of survival or distraction and rarely crimes of greed.

Take a look at Jean Valjean in *Les Misérables*, which is ultimately a story about a man who steals a loaf of bread and some candlesticks on account of being a bit hard up, becomes a sort of stepdad and then is hounded by the police state until he dies. Honestly, that could be half the boys I grew up with, but this was country Queensland so they were called Keith or Scott and there was no singing because singing is for poofs.

When you are of this social milieu, it doesn't matter whether you actually break the law or not. You are under the microscope because people who have grown up wealthy through greed can't help but project their motives onto those below them.

In the United States, the Internal Revenue Service (IRS) has conceded it audits poor people on their taxes more than it does for rich people. In some cases, up to 50 per cent more often than for people in well-heeled counties. That sounds silly. If they're after money, why not go after the wealthy ones? Turns out it's just too hard. You see, they have a shrinking budget and it's much easier for a junior burger at the IRS to audit the one-page tax return of a low-income worker than it is to go after the moderately rich who use trusts and shell companies to spread ownership of assets and resources, some of which can be and are registered in offshore tax havens like Guernsey or Bermuda or some island with three cows, a flock of sheep and 455 multinational companies all registered to one bungalow with a single room. You can't get a college grad on those cases, so often there is no one on them at all.

You might wonder what the spoils of war are in a campaign against people who have nothing. After all, wars are famously fought for things. Oil, land, money, being able to punch Nazis. And sure, sometimes you have to give those things back. Pay the damages, return the natural resources, apologise to the Nazis by creating a New World Order in which not only is fascism back but also where we have to be nice about it because God forbid they are subjected to some mean tweets while actively pursuing and destroying minorities and cultivating hate as a sort of toxic soil in which nothing but the most twisted politics can grow.

But what's to gain from going to town on people who have no fucking money?

Compliance by proxy. As Robert Hughes notes in *The Fatal Shore*, part of the genesis of the convicts being sent to Australia in the first place, sparking a chain of events that would try and fail to extinguish the oldest surviving civilisation on the planet, was fear of a new, united criminal underclass. As Hughes notes:

> The failure of language – the tyranny of moral generalisation over social inspection – fed the ruling class's belief that it was endangered from below.

I regret to inform you, things have not changed. The ruling class were worried, essentially, about revolution instead of casting a critical eye over the conditions that led to the crime waves that threatened property owners. There was no great outbreak of criminal enterprises or gangs as imagined by the middle and upper classes; they were being mugged by people who were starving and wanted to live.

Revolutions are rare because, for the most part, the system is designed to make every class on every rung of the ladder worry about the mob below them rather than the few at the very top. While a threshold proportion of people below the top of the ladder are preoccupied with the fear of those below them, the system stands.

To gerrymander this illusion, society must occasionally latch on to an individual's rags-to-riches story. Some people in my circumstances may even fall for their own magic trick, convinced that they escaped poverty because they put in the hard work and had the self-restraint required to make the correct decisions.

It's the fallacy of the one who made it out.

Here is a truth: taking one pig from the piggery and putting it on show tells us nothing about the lives of the others. We give you the show pig so that we don't have to talk about the ones that went to slaughter. Opportunity is, in theory, accessible to all. But we do not pay the same entry price.

Of course, we tell ourselves these stories because we believe having money is an intrinsic measure of worth, like the perfect kilogram which is stored in a vault outside of Paris and from which the weight has meaning.

For some, money is not just a measure of worth but of moral character. If you are able to look after yourself and your family, you are pure because you resisted temptation at every turn. Struggling? Totally impoverished? Congratulations. You're morally culpable for your own condition.

The mantra of Scott Morrison when he emerged as Prime Minister is instructive in this case. *If you have a go, you'll get a go.* Apart from the stultifying nothingness of the language deployed in that phrase, it simply isn't true. It wasn't accurate before he became the leader and it isn't now. The slogan appeals to a bias burrowed beneath the skin of people who have never known deep financial struggle; that it is the passivity of poor people that locks them in disadvantage. The only time they are ascribed agency or effort under such a regime is when they have 'done' something unhelpful like become addicted to drugs or taken on bad debt or married an abusive husband. Otherwise, and I'm paraphrasing the mindset here, they simply haven't had a go.

Anyone who has ever played a game of Monopoly can tell you there are no guarantees you'll come out the other side of it owning hotels on Mayfair and Park Lane. A crude analogy for a crude motto, perhaps, but if our leaders found themselves losing in a game, I imagine they would have quite a bit to say about the role of luck.

Rarely do we see the same messaging from the politicians who were taught to, or as a matter of instinct already do, worship at the altar of individual effort. In this telling of things, the individual alone is the illness and the cure. By the power vested in them, and ignoring all other interactions and the tangle of systems or institutions that complicate our lives, the single person has sole discretion about where to go in life, as if they have jumped into a taxi cab and simply rattled off a destination.

Such blind faith is why these same figures are left with no other explanation for working-age welfare recipients. It is literally inconceivable that anyone would stay on the below–poverty line payments (as they were before currently temporary boosts due to the coronavirus economic shock) if they didn't want to be there. Instead, they must all be dole bludgers with a thirst for the public teat. This nomenclature hints at the true meaning of 'have a go, get a go', which can be reduced to this: if you don't want to be poor, then don't be poor.

For some reason, this helpful advice reminds me of a time when I was in school and my friend and his parents, keen golfers all of them, were trying to teach me how to play. On the fifth hole I swung the putter and the ball raced past the hole. My friend Latham, with all the help he could muster, provided his assessment of my technique.

'You hit it too hard,' he said. Or: just don't be poor.

In a broader sense, this malignant thinking underpins the very idea of prosperity gospel. Such a religious model is not to say that God only loves you when you're rich, it's more insidious than that. Under this interpretation of the Bible, He makes you rich because He loves you; it is a reward for moral strength.

Mega churches in Australia have used this bootleg reading of the scriptures to make themselves very rich from their often middle-of-the-road followers. This, perversely, becomes proof of concept for the very idea of a deity that shows Her love the only way a good parent knows how: through bribery.

Perhaps I need not venture too far down this path, but let the record show: the most rudimentary understanding of the Bible shows us that Jesus hated, above all, the frauds, hawkers and charlatans at temple and spent more time hanging out with people in slums than an arts graduate on a voluntourism gap year. It is possible, though unlikely, that the scrolls containing 'The Gospel of Jesus and the Brexit Hedge Fund' or 'The Gospel Where Jesus Told Zacchaeus the Tax Collector That His Assets and Profits Were Offshored in Panama and Good Luck With That' are out there somewhere.

My point here is not a claim to religious instruction.

The scaffold for prosperity gospel indoctrination was here before the American televangelists bought their first Gulfstream jet. Their scam worked because deep down we believed it to be true.

You know, we judge people for the decisions they have made absent a total understanding of the forces at play. What appear to be choices to people with means are not so obvious or even possible for those without.

Take toilet paper.

Poor people pay more per roll of toilet paper than rich people because they can never afford, at one time, to buy the bulk pack of twenty-four.

This applies, too, for fruits and vegetables in food deserts; for other combo deals at supermarkets; for finance, on power bills if they miss the payments and on dental costs that add up over time because a single preventative visit is so expensive in this country.

We spend more on energy costs because we either can't afford to make our own homes more efficient or our landlords refuse to do it. Our work is also, on average, less secure and the intergenerational nature of poverty often means the tight spots are ours alone; there are no mums and dads or siblings or aunts and uncles coming to save us when the money monster lunges.

We have no guarantors for home loans. The guarantor in my world is as real as the Minotaur from Greek mythology. The body of a man, the head of an investment vehicle run by your parents.

It was Wittgenstein who said the borders of my language are the borders of my world. This was no mere rhetorical flourish. Time and again we see cultures who are able to express themselves in ways we have never imagined simply because they invented a word for something. But the philosopher might also have been talking about money, too, which cages us or sets us free in ways that are both immediate and long-lasting.

Indeed, we are bent out of shape by its force in ways we have yet to comprehend.

—

I want you to really, fully understand what growing up skint has meant for the development of me. And to do this, I need you to believe me when I say I am being as honest as I know how. This is not an absolution for personal responsibility, nor is it an endorsement. As ever, I find life to be far more complicated at the margins.

The absolutists are ideologues and getting an ideologue to explore the contours of our inner lives is like getting a cartographer to write down only the rivers and mountain ranges about which he feels strongly.

What a useless map that would be.

'Hey, this map doesn't have the Great Dividing Range on it,' I yell at my friend as we drive our car into a deposit of metamorphic dolomite rock about which we had no warning. 'If only this hadn't been drawn by conservative cartographer Mork Bullhorn who has a noted history favouring cap-rock ranges over multi-state formations that bisect the continent. How did he even get this job?'

I still prefer the taste of tinned pineapple, beetroot and peaches over the fresh variety.

That's a leftover of my childhood because buying that stuff brand new – you know, as a whole fruit – was simply out of the question. I got used to it. I was really confused when I heard the hype about the peach scene in *Call Me By Your Name* because I honestly thought Elio was going in on a tin of fruit which ended up making me feel sexually repressed.

Last week I spent $300 over two days and two locksmith visits rather than catch a train into the city to get a key from a friend who was staying with me for a few days. Despite telling him not to lock the bottom lock of the door, he did, twice, and I didn't have the heart to break it to him that he had locked me out of my house.

On both occasions I had returned home from a day trip away so there was also the element of expediency: I just wanted to go to bed. Before I earned enough money to hide the idiocy of the world I had come to inhabit, the locksmith simply wasn't an option. I would have had to wait hours, or catch a bus for two hours return or spend the night on a friend's couch before getting my life back.

This sounds silly. But to me, the guy who now has enough money to be temporarily comfortable, it is not silly. I would sooner spend that cash on anything that doesn't remind me of the effort it took to live in my early 20s than save it for a day that might not come. I would sooner spend that money on things that feel good right now because my brain, and by extension myself, will do whatever it takes to avoid the reminder of that past.

Colouring my behaviour as an adult is what I witnessed as a child. I saw Mum's daily, sometimes hourly, battles to stay solvent. I saw how hard she worked and what it did to her body and her mind. The stress of even thinking about it now is difficult to explain. It is built not only into my own mind but also in my flesh. The things I will do to avoid that feeling today. The things I try to do for Mum to make it so that she never has to feel it again.

By my late twenties, these feelings had become imprinted. My friend told me to read a collection of essays by the American writer Samantha Irby, specifically because Irby's relationship to money was absurd and I reminded my friend of her.

'So I have that disease that a lot of poor people who claw their way out of the miserable depths of poverty suffer from, the one that makes you want to blow your pay check on all the special things because never before in your life could you ever have had anything even remotely fancy or expensive,' Irby writes in *We Are Never Meeting in Real Life*.

Been there, detonated that.

Of marriage, Irby says:

What I really need is someone who remembers to rotate this meaty pre-corpse toward the sun every couple of days and tries to get me to stop spending my money like a goddamn NBA lottery pick.

I think my friend told me about this book when I was seriously discussing buying a cocktail cabinet from an antique store down the road.

'Why do you need to get a cocktail cabinet,' she said.

I thought about it for half a second.

'Because I need to get rid of my money.'

This is not the kind of thinking that will be awarded a Nobel Prize. It is the kind of thinking that will see me give US$240 and possibly my credit card details to some album scammers in New York's Times Square on the vanishingly small chance that the men genuinely needed my help.

There is a sense of fatalism at play, here.

Another friend told me about her husband, also raised by a single mother in the grip of financial struggle, who would never retrieve loose change if he dropped it in the street. When the couple moved house, she (from a middle-class background) realised he had no intention of taking a jar of change to the bank. It mortified her and raised barely a register of understanding in him. She took the jar to the bank and cashed the couple of hundred dollars it contained. But what was all that about?

I understood. He, like me, never felt he had any real control over his life. Neither the dropped coins nor the jar of shrapnel could, or would, make a great dent in the structural misfortune of his existence, so why bother? This isn't an argument for throwing away your money, but it is a perception wired into the mind of every kid who came from nowhere. If fate has marked its intentions so clearly, resistance to its motives is effort that can scarcely be spared. Hope takes many forms in these lives but it is a disfigured, pragmatic kind of thing. From a distance it may even resemble hopelessness. Remember, this is a symptom in people who are from poverty but on the way out, even marginally. It is a psychological leftover. The opposite is true when you are in the teeth of penury.

I know from watching Mum, and living my early adult years, that enough five-cent coins can buy a meal. Perhaps that is why I hated them so much when I scratched my way into luck and promise later on. It was like kicking a habit. I felt ashamed to buy anything with five-cent pieces and I never wanted to see them again. Good riddance.

All of these hang-ups carry financial penalties. Of course, I am lucky that I managed to muddle into a life that allows me to absorb the shocks. When I first moved to Canberra for work, I didn't own a car. I could have caught a bus to work but the idea filled me with dread. So I spent $600 a month on taxis instead. Is that a wise investment? Hell no. At least, not if you measure it only in financial terms. Was it something I deemed necessary? My word.

You see, I have my own mental health problems. Some of them have stemmed from that unending quest for security, others from the trauma of being cast aside by one of the people who should have loved me and never found ways in which he could.

I spend money to eliminate the stressors that are within my control, a tactic that allows me to better fight the ones that aren't.

Last year I received the first instalment of an advance for another book I am writing. It was more money than I have ever seen in my bank account at one time. The bank portal has a wee little graph that charts the previous twenty transactions on a line. It went from flatlining at zero dollars to an almost vertical line in one day. And it made me feel sick. Actually physically sick.

I joked to a friend, Perry, that I would have to flee the country because it was too much money and he said to me: 'See, this is how we know you were poor. You think that amount of money is worth skipping the country for.'

And then I spent it. And I know why I spent it.

All those years staring at a bank account that sits below zero – like the investors watching their money literally freeze during Robert Falcon Scott's expedition to the South Pole – wires the brain to expect blank space. Money was never the default option in my world, it was the exception to the rule.

More crucially, people without financial security, but especially their children, are conditioned to understand one inalienable fact about the world in which they live: money doesn't hang around. If it's not a phone bill, it'll be an unplanned trip to the mechanic or a late payment fee, the dentist, a hike in rent.

In this environment, when rare financial windfalls happen – like a better-than-expected tax return – it might be prudent to put some away for a rainy day. But think about that for just one second, from that person's point of view. If the thing keeping you in place is bigger than any one financial decision, if it is bigger than you are, what mercy the small deferrals? The money will go, whether you put it in the rent fund or buy a new TV. It will go, one way or another.

When you are at or near the bottom, the race to survive is brutal. In this state, prioritising short-term distractions over long-term solvency isn't madness. It makes perfect sense. You've lived the long-term already and it rarely works out in your favour.

What use is the rainy day fund when it is torrential every day?

So when I hear commentators bemoaning the fact that poor people seem to have new televisions or phones, there is only one thought that springs to mind. Why won't you shut the fuck up?

I mean, what did you want them to do? Jettison every last skerrick of comfort or ease? Should they lean into the misery of it all, like a joyless windsock? Such a life is like driving along a new road at night. You can see the white lines dividing the bitumen in the headlights, but you've no idea what comes next. There is no sense of a future, no mind map of the whole journey. Just one white line after another in the dark.

Money is a force that acts on us, contracting time and space.

To that end, I have spent every dollar I have ever earned. There have been no savings. My bank account number was committed to memory well over a decade ago, because of the countless times I have had to borrow money from friends to see me through my own blundering psychology. It is money spent in the now, the only time I've been able to conceptualise. In my early 20s, with the attendant psychodramas of self-discovery and the onset of complex post-traumatic stress disorder, I honestly didn't think I would, and didn't plan to, live past the age of thirty.

Unpicking the stitches of that ridiculous tapestry is no easy thing. Would that it were so.

As the Peloponnesian War finally ended and the great warriors of Sparta released the city of Athens back to its own people, Athenian pride had taken a hit. But so diffuse was the ethos of the extraordinary among them that they pardoned their invaders and allowed them to stay on as citizens. The rhetoricians ran around Athens, congratulating themselves.

'The Spartans may win wars, but nobody does defeat like the Athenians!'

I liked this way of looking at things. As a young man who was unsure of the hand he had been given, it had a frisson of hope about it. Defeat sounds harsh and uninviting, but it was ours.

Acceleration, both as a physical force and class mobility, can weigh you down. The further you manage to claw your way into relative comfort, the more distant the life behind you. Very near the start of this journey there is a fulcrum, as in a seesaw, which will tip the class traveller most assuredly into a kind of danger.

It is at this point that the risks of this uncharted territory outweigh the ability of those we've left behind to rescue us. For me, it was a credit card. But there are jobs and social situations and scrapes or assorted other debts; cultural vortexes and, God, politics that will be entirely alien to those who, for whatever reason, have been unable to climb out onto the same road.

There are risks in most ventures, certainly. I want to be clear, though, that nothing feels as lonely or out of reach as this waypoint between two worlds. As an eighteen year old moving 100 kilometres away for work and university, I had rent and obligations. I had a constellation of expectations that, before I had even reached my twenties, outstripped those experienced by my mother in her entire life. Failure here, at this particular juncture, would have had profound consequences for the man I wanted to be and the boy I no longer was.

More importantly, it would have muted the only hope we had that Mum's sacrifice might have been for something.

One of my favourite accomplishments of humankind – alongside the trackless tram (it's just a bus) and lay-by – is the launch of the Voyager 1 and 2 spacecraft in 1977. The two hunks of metal and probes are now the farthest man-made objects from planet Earth.

Since 2011, when Voyager 1 was about sixteen light-hours away from Earth, I've been following a Twitter account that simply tweets daily updates on how far both craft are from home. It takes light from the sun just eight minutes to reach us here on the blue planet. In 2012, Voyager 1 burst into interstellar space. The second craft managed the same feat in 2019.

On my last check in, the first spacecraft is now 20 hours, 35 minutes and 50 seconds of light-travel time from Earth. Tracking these updates has become somewhat of an obsession, partly, I think, because I have anthropomorphised these spacecraft and imagined their loneliness.

It now takes the better part of a day to send or retrieve signals from them. If, by some infinitesimally small chance, they were hit by space rock and wiped out, it would take almost twenty-one hours to know about it.

That is what it feels like to move from nothing to something.

The emptiness of it. The peril. So far from home, yet having arrived nowhere.

I turned thirty-three recently, an auspicious occasion because it made me the same age as Jesus of Nazareth when he was crucified and, similarly, neither of us were home owners.

Something has changed in the last year, however. I can see more than the immediate road markings in front of me. I have what feels like a future. Maybe even a happy one. I have laid some ghosts to rest, and I have done two of the major things I wanted to do for my mum before I set about trying to buy my own apartment.

Helping Mum, in itself, was a mission.

Last year I paid for a $14,000 renovation of my mum's bathroom. The one she had was Dickensian in its presentation and about as practical as her gay son. Its time really had come.

The walls were panelled in a pale green asbestos cement sheet called Tilux, a product manufactured by James Hardie and used with vigour in Australian homes between the 1950s and 1970s. Linoleum covered the floors. Put together, the room had the visual aesthetic of an abandoned asylum.

In my push to give her only the nicest things, we immediately clashed. Mum wanted a rainfall showerhead and I embarked on a mission to get her the largest rainfall showerhead in south-east Queensland. Deb was perfectly happy with the 250-millimetre round head but the largest I found in the store was 400 millimetres.

I wanted her to have that one. I wanted her to have the best one. That means the biggest one; the most expensive. I wanted a fitting that would block out the sun or, under the right conditions, pick up microwave background radiation from space.

She tried reasoning with me but I wouldn't be moved. She is our family saviour, the little Hobbit who could, and it must be so.

'I just think that one might be too big, darl,' she pleaded with me.

'You wanted a rainfall shower though,' I said. 'This will really make it rain!'

'That one will wash me down the drain.'

It wasn't until I fished the thing out of its box that I realised how truly absurd I was being. It was the size of a manhole cover, so it seemed, and would have looked comically out of place. Mum won.

Still, on other items she went reflexively for the cheapest option. And every time, I had a conversation with her that went like this: 'I don't know if you really like that one the most. If you do, we can get it. But if you are only choosing it because it is the least expensive then I want you to stop and pick the one you like the most.'

This was new territory for us. How do we learn to trust this expansion of our borders? How will it change us?

I bought Mum a car for Christmas, nothing flash but also nothing that would break down on the side of a road or attract the attention of the police. It had been five years since she had owned a car because there was just no way of piecing the savings together in the first place, let alone meeting the repair bills.

To be without a vehicle in a country town with literally no public transport – no way in or out, no bus or train or horse-drawn coach – is to lack freedom. A year or so after the last car was sold for $100 of scrap, Mum told me that she was buying a little pink grocery trolley that she could pull on the 1.5-kilometre round-trip walk up town to buy food and cat litter. Of course I made jokes about it, and pretended my horror, but this masked a deeper concern that neither of us wanted to talk about.

'You're too young for a grandma trolley,' I told her at the time.

She was in her mid-fifties.

'Plus,' I said, 'it's embarrassing.'

That wasn't the issue, of course. I was ashamed at myself for not having the money on hand to help Mum in a more material way. It was maddening that this was where things had ended up for both of us; this gulf between the life she lived and the one that was slowly revealing itself to me. She coped, as she has always done, with good grace and meticulous planning. We slipped into our usual routine of telling bad jokes about the situation.

My job has always been to make Deb laugh, even though she has never requested it. Our collective sense of humour runs on the fumes of struggle and injustice. From the outside it would seem inappropriate, macabre.

We could afford laughter.

The decision to buy Mum the car was slow and then very fast. I thought perhaps I had missed the Christmas 2019 deadline until I arrived on December 24 and realised the banks were still open and I could get my sister Lauryn's more expert advice on the make and model. We walked into the Bendigo Bank branch in Boonah, where I had started the only bank account I've ever used in Year 9, and asked to withdraw the $7000 needed for the purchase in cash.

At first, the bank teller was not impressed.

'Did you call ahead and reserve the money?' she asked.

'No,' I told her. 'I didn't know that was a thing. This is a bank, right? I thought you had money here.'

I wasn't trying to be difficult. It had just never occurred to me, nor had I the need to discover that there is only so much of the printed stuff to go around. Thankfully they had enough out back and the teller took us into a meeting room where she began counting the bundle of 50s and 100s.

'I've never seen this much money in my life,' I said to Lauryn as it was all laid out on the table. She was taking photos and filming me on her phone. 'Well, except at a drug bust,' I added.

The teller stopped counting and gave me a strange look. It was the kind of look that said 'I've made a huge mistake.' I knew it well, from having made it many times myself.

'I'm a journalist,' I said. 'I meant, at drug busts that I have covered.'

It felt like a relief to hand the money over when we picked up the car in Brisbane that afternoon, and not simply because it was a stack of cash that could easily have been misplaced. It was a relief precisely because it felt weird having that kind of money at all, whether it was coded digitally in my bank balance or existing as a brick of notes in my pocket. Liquidity was not part of my normal, no matter how I understood the need for resources on an intellectual level.

When the panic buying ahead of the coronavirus shutdown began in March the next year, I thought again of Mum and that car. She used to rely on getting some of the bigger grocery items delivered via one of the major supermarkets 40 kilometres away. It was more expensive but Deb had an old leg injury that never healed, in part because she couldn't get in to see a specialist for two months. The walk up town was painful and slow. Then food disappeared from the shelves and these deliveries were suspended for all but the most urgent of cases. Even with the car, it was a complete lottery in the local country town grocery store as to what was available each day.

Just three months earlier and she would have been trundling up town with her 'gammy leg' for a shot at buying the essentials of living and no guarantees. I was flushed with a combination of gratefulness that she was not in that position and guilt that the only reason she wasn't was because my own station in life had changed. I felt ashamed that so much had to go right in my own life just for something to not fail in hers.

There was shame, too, that I seemed to have squandered so much of that luck.

Researchers from Harvard, Princeton and the University of Warwick and University of British Columbia, among countless others, have done the work on understanding these apparently counterintuitive psychological models of money. Poor people are actually closer to model economic citizens when faced with scarcity. They think more deeply and at greater cognitive costs – in some studies, the stress led to real-world hits of up to 13 IQ points on the mind of someone engaged in solving a financial problem – than those for whom the stakes are not so high. Abundance, on the other hand, engages us too little.

If you combine the effects of moving from one to the other, from nothing to more than enough, then you are left with someone who looks a lot like me. Currently, or at least most of the time these days, I have no reason to fear my card being declined at the shops. And yet, I am still seized by the tension of each moment when I go to pay for something.

Statistically, I will need to live a lot longer for the balance sheet to be reversed on that one. The hyper-vigilance required around money – Is there enough? Will there be enough? What payments are coming out and when? – has nowhere to go, now. Nowhere useful, anyhow. It lives on as a general threat assessment, constantly running a thousand different models about how all this comfort could be undone.

If you spent your childhood and early adult years in a state of survival, the brain remembers. A bank balance can come good after much effort, but, later in life, the architecture of the mind can't be so easily bought.

Money can, however, buy a lot of things for which there are never transactions. This is on the proviso that you have it and can be shaped by its presence from an early age.

Without money ever changing hands, it can make you confident. The very idea of your access to it, if needed, is performance-enhancing. Because we attach worth to income or wealth, people who are not raised with the insulation of money can come to see their own ideas as being without value. Certainly, in my case, it took me well over a decade into adulthood before I began to accept that maybe I had something worth saying. And I don't mean that I was searching to become the 'voice of a generation' or someone with the great Australian novel burrowing out from their skin. I mean it in the very ordinary sense of being in a group of people, many of whom are better educated or middle class or rich or from family money, and being unable or unwilling to attach value to my own worldview.

This phenomenon becomes worse the more you move into a world that wasn't meant for you. University was just the start. Later, the media. Or law. Or politics. Medicine. Some people have a head start in the contest of ideas, and rarely does it have anything to do with the intrinsic worth of those ideas. They are just better at voicing them, forcefully at times, and defending them. I have lost count of the number of times I've interviewed people who are on government payments or out of work and really struggling, who have apologised to me for being unable to articulate the nature of their concerns.

But here's the thing. With almost no exceptions, they spoke plain and true. Their thinking was not polluted with pretence or the preening addition of academic theory, nor did they feel the need to furnish their thoughts with complicated clauses or, God forbid, allegories. What they lacked was confidence.

You might argue that these are deficits of cultural access, not money, but that would ignore the relationship between the two. In many cases, they are one and the same.

To have money is to constantly be playing a game. It's more of a facade than the consequential battle for survival that consumes people with nothing, but it is a prison of its own kind.

I was having coffee with a friend recently who was telling me about how he seemed less guarded than most of the other people in his line of work. He was more personally honest, sometimes in a way that shocked his colleagues.

'That's a money thing,' I told him. 'If you've got something, you've got something to lose. So they never give too much away.'

Me, on the other hand. I've always worked on the premise that anything is worth a try.

Writing at the extreme end of poverty, Marlon James describes life in the fictionalised Jamaican ghetto of Copenhagen City and the Eight Lanes in *A Brief History of Seven Killings*. It is a line I come back to often because it has an elemental truth to it.

And I see the zinc on the roof rust itself
brown, and then the rain batter hole into it
like foreign cheese, and I see seven people
in one room and one pregnant and people
fucking anyway because people so poor that
they can't even afford shame and I wait.

Just a few lines later, James describes Bam-
Bam's idea of trying to escape the coarse
penury in which he lives but both Copenhagen
City and the Eight Lanes are 'too big and every
time you reach the edge, the edge move ahead
of you like a shadow until the whole world is
ghetto'.

It does feel a bit like that as you grow older,
even if the ghetto only lives on in your mind.
You drag it with you and it colours reality.

Tech entrepreneur Ricky Yean writes about the 'bugs' in the coding of his own brain that came from relentless stress and the worry of childhood poverty.

'Then there's the issue of knowing how to manage resources. Being poor makes you suck at using money as a resource. My time was always cheaper growing up, so I got used to opting to spend time rather than money,' he says in Quartz.

If you didn't have much growing up, chances are you know how to stretch a dollar. That's adaptive. What few of us learn, however, is how to turn one dollar into two or four or five million. Money is a resource but some of us, by osmosis or direct instruction, never understand how fully it can be tapped.

And that's important. The wealth gap in Australia is widening. The prime mover in this respect is not income but assets, overwhelmingly accumulated by older generations and gaining value at rates that have helped blow the margin right out. Housing and superannuation have been the key sources of wealth but, as the Grattan Institute noted in its 2019 report on generational wealth, these gains are unlikely to be repeated for younger people.

'All but the richest households headed by someone younger than 35 have lower real net wealth in 2016 than similar households in 2004,' the report says.

And while well-off younger people in 2016 have more wealth than their counterparts in 2004, these gains are dwarfed by those of households over 65, right across the wealth spectrum.

Home-ownership rates are also dropping fastest for the young and the poor. In 1981, 60 per cent of people in the lowest wealth quintile aged 25–34 owned a home. Today the figure is just 20 per cent. In other words, wealth gaps are growing within most generations as well as between them, and the gaps within generations are particularly large for young people. The intergenerational transfer of wealth via inheritances will only exacerbate this problem.

Money makes money.

In the funhouse mirror of inequity, existing features are exaggerated. The wealth gains of the past four decades are increasingly gobbled up by those who already had the most. Wage growth was consistently flat ahead of the second global shock in twelve years that arrived with the coronavirus pandemic. It is the deepest, broadest and most terrifying economic crisis since the Great Depression, and it is also the event that will finally spell the end of the hope that young Australians could have maintained the trend of earning more than the generation that came before it. Now that is gone, too.

The Grattan researchers point out that these are entire age groups and, within them, the range of those who are wildly successful and those who are struggling to feed themselves or pay the electricity bill is vast. But even with those ranges, there is no mistaking the asset-propelled near-trebling of wealth among those aged 65 to 75 since 1994. Young people in the 25 to 34 age bracket increased their net wealth by an average of just 57 per cent.

This isn't really a story about the wealth gap, however, but I need you to understand the scale at which precarity has seized the lives of the poorest and particularly the youngest.

As this march continues, the already leaden government approach to welfare policy in Australia becomes more obscene. In just the most recent example, the Commonwealth presided over an automated 'debt' recovery programme for more than half a decade that it knew, or had every indication it needed, was illegal. Robodebt averaged incomes in a way that could never have matched reality and now the Coalition has announced it will pay back some three-quarters of a billion dollars to more than 370,000 people.

This is likely to be just a pinch of what is actually owed, not including damages. Nor will this enormous figure remedy affairs for those who were so emotionally and financially brittle when these algorithmic debt notices were sent that they killed themselves. This was a large-scale government programme that embezzled money from the poorest people in Australia.

There is plenty of evidence that technology allowed data-matching in the welfare space to improve 'compliance' programmes over fifteen years, purportedly raking in more money each budget cycle. Often, however, these initiatives cost more money to implement than they brought in as revenue. I first reported on increased medical checks for the Disability Support Pension (DSP) that was eventually abandoned because, *quelle surprise*, almost everybody already receiving the higher-rate DSP was meant to be there.

What does this tell us, then?

It was never about the money. There has been no effort to understand the psychology of bare-knuckle survival. Rather, a prodigious, emotionally barren attempt at blame and punishment has taken root. Oh, it's been a long time coming. And, like the foundations of prosperity gospel, we have allowed it to happen because many of us believe in the atomic truth of the proposals: that money measures worth and moral character. Those who have it don't just appear to be more important, they are more important. The effect is the same as gaining mass in the rising elevator, or time in the rocket ship travelling near the speed of light. But remember this: the importance is attached to the money, not the person. Most often these people are more easily listened to, more readily approved and justifiably integral to society because they can buy the ears of those who would listen, purchase the things for which approval is given and partake in the multiple transactions of modern life that make them so indispensable.

I have come to realise that most people don't talk about money the way Mum and I speak about money.

How much is it? That's the question that governed our every waking moment. Whether we had to say it out loud or not, it bounced around the cavity in our skulls.

People of certain means don't discuss such affairs because they have no need for it. It costs what it costs. Of course they might mention how much they paid for a new home – maybe – but, in comparison, we asked this about Snickers bars and Pizza Pockets and electricity and movie tickets.

That's our brains at work again. *How much is it?* was the question we asked when we were figuring out how.

Of course if lack of money warps our brains, where is the evidence that too much of it does the same for rich people?

I don't want to be mean, but have you seen rich people? They behave like they turned up to a fancy dress Gatsby-themed birthday party and then never went home. Laws become mere guidelines and actual guidelines, like those road markings, become suggestions.

Rich people are like toddlers. You might get a good one. Most of them might even be well meaning. But when it comes down to it, they are weird little people, and you should keep an eye on them.

There are studies in the United States that show low-income people are more likely than not to stop for pedestrians at a zebra crossing.

High-net-worth individuals, however, are as likely as not to do the same.

Drink that in for a minute.

There are extreme cases to illustrate any point we care to make here, but take the now dead paedophile sex-trafficker Jeffrey Epstein. Here was a man with unfathomable wealth who used it and the powerful people that attach themselves to it to orchestrate not only a decades-long under-age rape pyramid scheme but the initial sweetheart deal that saw dozens of charges dropped in favour of a vanishingly small penalty.

He went to jail for eighteen months for the crime of soliciting prostitution, but even then he was on a work-release programme six days a week and came and went with impunity from his Palm Beach mansion during the day. Jail for Epstein the first time around was more akin to a shabby motel where he was required to sleep at night.

Jeffrey Epstein was not more important than his victims. The substrate of the world in which he lived, however, was materially different and it allowed him to bend the laws of physics, and human laws, just as gravity does. In this manner, his world was structurally different and the warping of time and space governed the behaviour of everyone in his orbit.

If you allow it, wealth creates a moral slipstream in which the man or woman in possession of great fortune can travel. People without means can be immoral too, but, like everything, they usually have to work much harder at it.

In his timeless essay 'In Praise of Idleness', Bertrand Russell wrote with sparkling clarity about a problem that persists to this day.

'The idea that the poor should have leisure has always been shocking to the rich,' he writes.

In England in the early nineteenth century fifteen hours was the ordinary day's work for a man; children sometimes did as much, and very commonly did twelve hours a day. When meddlesome busy-bodies suggested that perhaps these hours were rather long, they were told that work kept adults from drink and children from mischief.

When I was a child, shortly after urban working men had acquired the vote, certain public holidays were established by law, to the great indignation of the upper classes. I remember hearing an old Duchess say, 'What do the poor want with holidays? They ought to work.' People nowadays are less frank, but the sentiment persists, and is the source of much economic confusion.

Elsewhere, Russell laments that the necessity of preaching the dignity of work to the poor – so that they may be contented – has been done for thousands of years by the rich 'while taking care themselves to remain undignified in this respect'.

The system of mutual obligations in the current Australian welfare system would appear to reanimate that point. It is simply not enough to provide a safety net that allows those unfortunate souls to scrape by; it must also come with a legislated requirement for labour. Work for the Dole is just one element of the programme. Despite the fact that businesses hate it, welfare recipients must also search and apply for up to twenty jobs every month and attend frequently pointless 'training' sessions with outsourced employment service providers for the privilege of being kept on the margins.

Russell wouldn't have been surprised to learn the $7 billion employment services industry – which survives on placement bonuses that the worst providers harass out of clients who find work on their own anyway – is perfectly at home with leisure. Their own employees are, of course, overworked, but the organisations themselves do the bare minimum to enforce a regime that can never forgive idleness on the part of the broke citizens in its clutch.

The system is so preoccupied with whether the poor are getting something for 'free' that it has a multi-billion-dollar apparatus of non-government and private organisations taking the absolute piss and making money all the while. To borrow from Douglas Adams, these are companies and businesses who would – were they ever to question the nature of their own existence – vanish in a puff of logic.

As we've already shown, it is a myth that those without money, or even work, are idle.

There is more kinetic energy in the life of struggle than the life of means. The mistake we make is confusing actual hard work with the work money can perform for us.

This, I think, is the intellectual poison of wealth. Here, money is like one of those hulking robotic exoskeletons being developed for soldiers in war. The prototypes convert the ordinary abilities of a single human and make them five or ten times as powerful. With one of these things on, you could lift a car. People with money are people with exoskeletons and, given enough time, it can be easy to assume the strength is yours alone and not simply on loan from a mechanic suit.

Are you really good at cleaning or do you just have a cleaner? And so on.

I was staying at a fancy hotel in Sydney for a work event one evening last year and I had driven in from Canberra. That end of town always sets my nerves on fire so I just drove into the main hotel driveway and paid $75 for overnight valet. It was the first time in my life I had ever done so. I gave my keys to the valet and then, after simultaneously apologising and saying thank you twenty times, I walked away.

And then it hit me. If you're rich – like, really rich – you don't even have to park your own car! This is just one example, of course. If you've enough cash, you can do this for laundry and ironing and maintenance. A friend of mine at university, who happened to be the heiress to a billion-dollar Greek shipping fortune, was a member of a 24/7 online concierge service for the ultra rich. She just told them what she wanted to do and they arranged everything for her. No task too small.

What must that do to a person? Somebody should put them in an fMRI scanner and find out.

My argument here doesn't turn on jealousy. At the strange, exclusive university to which I was awarded a scholarship (and a cadetship as a journalist) I encountered truly, stupidly rich people for the first time. One of them, whose dad was worth $250 million, kept me as a sort of pet and would show me off as this kid from the arse-end of nowhere and nothing.

He would rub his belly after lavishly shouting everyone dinner and say things like

'Oh, I'm as full as a public school!' Then, a fortnight later, he would ask everyone to pay him back.

Honestly, it looked exhausting. I don't think he, or many of the others I knew there, had any true friends. I didn't envy them but the flagrant jockeying on wealth and status did spark something in me for the first time: a recognition that things were uneven. Look, I knew some people had more money than others and even we had more money than the poorest people in the country town where we settled. I was aware that there was an amplitude between those with the most and those with the least; it just didn't seem particularly big to young eyes. Give or take, we all just did our thing.

University, and my admission to the world at large, changed that for me. What I thought to be a gully was a canyon.

In Australia, many people feel like they are not earning enough money. Funnily enough, this is especially true the more you earn in the middle to upper-middle income bands. Turns out, seeing other people in your wealth quintile (a contender for my favourite word) buy things you can't yet afford yourself is a major driver of this feeling. In some surveys, one-fifth of people earning $200,000 a year thought they would need to make another $10,000 each week to feel rich. Some thought $20,000 extra each week might do the trick. At this point it might simply be easier to shoot an endangered species for sport and call it a day.

For context, the typical (median) Australian taxpayer earns $45,811. The average Australian earns $61,252. The overwhelming majority – 90 per cent – earn less than $117,000. So to be fair to those on 200-large or more, it's not like they're stratospherically out of touch with the masses, right? Ten per cent is still a crowd.

I have seen the entitlement of wealth from within my own family, too. The part that disowned us all and, in a strange way, saved us.

I have often said the same thing to Mum over the years. We never saw a cent of my violent grandfather George Morton's largesse, and many of his children didn't even end up with cattle stations because he died with a $6 million tax bill, which was, true to his vicious style, the final act of bastardry against them all.

The horror of having to make your own way in the world.

How cosmically calming it must be, I said to Mum, to move through life knowing – or at least believing – you have some huge inheritance coming to save you from your missteps. Maybe it makes you more adventurous, more willing to take risks. Certainly it creates a layer of protection, which might explain why so many people spend these inheritances in their head long before a loved one dies. And if the will is disputed, or changed, watch how they fight.

They fight because they suddenly land in a world that poor people have become adept at navigating; they thrash because the floor of the ocean has fallen away from their feet.

They are introduced, for the first time, to the friction of a life without clear access to money.

Money is a force that changes time and space. It can induce claustrophobia when it suddenly disappears.

There are essentially two ways a person experiences poverty: they can be born into it or thrust into it, by sudden and horrific changes in circumstances. For my family, it was the latter.

So many others have done it worse or had similar experiences. So many have been buffeted by trauma and addiction and disadvantage and in these lives we must acknowledge: the choices available to people like my family were never the same as the choices other people were able to make. There was one rule: survival. Everything else was secondary. For those born into poverty and the scarred lives of their parents, the structural factors are even more significant.

Choices. It's a strange slur from those above, isn't it. It's like yelling at a woman in the jaws of a lion that she should have gone to night classes. Or watching a man drown and saying, 'Well, I'm not going to rescue you, you should teach yourself to swim.'

That drowning man? Imagine telling him that he should just kick his feet. After all, that's what you did. Only, the man has concrete boots on and you had flippers. Or, if you were really privileged, a trained dolphin and an EPIRB beacon.

I am sick of the charade we have played in this country for so long now.

We are given platitudes about fortitude, never about the luck that so often paints our fate.

I dreamed of being rich when I was a kid. In my then estimation, that amounted to being able to afford a laptop and a house. The idea of having a laptop on which I could write anywhere at any time occupied so many of my waking moments that it became an obsession. Imagine the novels I could write! The essays!

How embarrassing it would be to go back in time and explain to that boy that I now have two laptops, an iPad and a phone on which I make and keep most of my notes for writing. How unedifying it is to admit that my own view of money has changed over time, to see it not so much as a luxury as I did then but as a necessity that has the power to split time and space.

I wonder now if I can get a graph of my bank balance going back to 2001 when I opened the account. What can such a line tell us about a person?

I don't want to be rich anymore but I do want something more extravagant. I want to be able to bend time and space so powerfully as to reverse it, to take back all of the moments that caused my mum to suffer and struggle and replay them with money. I want her to have been, *to be*, comfortable.

'I just wish I could win the lotto,' she says to me, still.

One day I stopped her.

'Maybe you already did. Maybe we're your lottery,' I said.

It wasn't offered in the syrupy 'love is your wealth' kind of way, though of course that is also true. Rather, I meant it in the sense I have come to understand as an adult. We will support you. Our money is yours, too. Because it will take money.

Yes, it will take much more hard work to make it compared to people who started with something. But hard work alone will not deliver us unto financial freedom. That's the thing about a lottery.

Everyone thinks they can win.

They cannot.

Read
'On'

Little Books,
Big Ideas

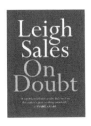

'A superbly stylish and valuable
little book on this century's great
vanishing commodity.'
Annabel Crabb

Acclaimed journalist Leigh Sales has her doubts, and
thinks you should, too. Her classic personal essay
carries a message about the value of truth, scrutiny and
accountability – a much-needed, pocket-sized antidote
to fake news.

Donald Trump, the post-truth world and the instability
of Australian politics are all examined in this fresh take
on her prescient essay on the media and political trends
that define our times.

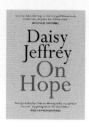

'Next-gen leaders like Daisy are showing us the way and their voices are only getting louder. We should listen.' Mike Cannon-Brookes

How ordinary people can change the world and help save the planet.

As extreme weather becomes the norm, scientists agree that our climate is changing. But it seems too many of our leaders aren't listening to the science and are failing to act.

In *On Hope*, one of the lead organisers of the Australian Climate strike, 17-year-old Daisy Jeffrey shows how ordinary people are fighting back and demanding we address climate change to help save our planet.

'This is the book we all need right now. Gemmell
nails how to achieve serenity and calm amid all the
crazy busyness of modern living.'
Lisa Wilkinson

International bestselling author Nikki Gemmell
writes on the power of quiet in today's shouty world.

Quiet comes as a shock in these troubled times.

Quietism means 'devotional contemplation and
abandonment of the will … a calm acceptance of things
as they are'. Gemmell makes the case for why quiet is
steadily gaining ground in this noisy age: Why we need
it now more than ever. How to glean quiet, hold on to it,
and work within it.

Katharine
Murphy
On
Disruption

The internet has shaken the foundations of life: public and private lives are wrought by the 24-hour, seven-day-a-week news cycle that means no one is ever off duty.

On Disruption is a report from the coalface of that change: what has happened, will it keep happening, and is there any way out of the chaos?

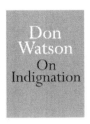

Don
Watson
On
Indignation

Don Watson takes us on a journey of indignation and how it has been expressed in his forebears. His ire towards US politicians has a new moving target: Donald Trump.

The US President's primary pitch had less to do with giving people money or security than it was about vengeance. Trump exploited the anger we feel when we are slighted or taken for granted, turning the politics of a sophisticated democracy into something more like a blood feud. He promised to restore their dignity, slay their enemies, re-make the world according to old rites and customs. He stirred their indignation into tribal rage and rode it into the White House.

It was a scam, of course, but wherever there is indignation, lies and stupidity abound.

hachette
AUSTRALIA

If you would like to find out more about
Hachette Australia, our authors, upcoming
events and new releases you can visit
our website or our social media channels:

hachette.com.au
HachetteAustralia
HachetteAus